MW01504631

Manifest

ISBN 978-0-9888776-2-7

Artwork and Poetry by Christina Perez-El

Editing by Christina Perez-El

Printed at:

The Detroit Impression Company, Inc.

1111 Bellevue St.

Detroit, MI 48207

(313) 784-9292

www.detroitprinter.net

This book details an ethereal relationship over the span of two years. This collection features the artist within her most vulnerable confessions.

Table of Contents

MANIFEST

Some things stay only

in dreams I wish for a scene

To touch what I've seen

Lips, face and hand grip

 Hair In an embrace show All

the loving ways you

fire of souls unite

you taught me how to stop All

the world in its tracks

Flying into an

Upward Spiral infinite

Love to be shown now

Mindful Prosthetics

An elegant smile
Shoulder length hair
How you turned your gaze away
                        from her
      To show direction point

      Part of your mission?
Maybe.
But to tell me that you wanted more babies?
to show age and talk about phasin' me?
& to think I followed your lead
when from her limbs she bleeds
from a need
of *your* hands
This is what you would not reveal
                     A caution of
               protection
I never save a confession
You found me sought me spoke to me
Lovely telepathy
Then when I go to materialize
Your endeavor
You cross me out, hide a name & push

Return to sender

Return to sender
Return to sender

Man with a gun

out of the church

straight ahead

quickly, hurry quick

sideways gaze

shield your face with the weapon and keep the other aimed in front of you

only Allah knows the danger ahead

so run

protected

"Keep GOING!"

An angry instruction

A yell into the atmosphere following

a panic in "UM....There's been a change in plans!"

cast the blame in the form of an uttered blade

I'm used to the shade

In the Sun I run until I've reached my destina-

SHUN

SHUN

SHONE.

Moon Lake

What if I told you

I didn't want to speak right now

not up for it

& all the eyes of scrutiny

So out to the large full moon

Which somehow you managed to pull

To Our Sight

The waters softly sing a reflection

Of the pale pearl light

Sitting at my side you reply,

"Be patient

with yourself."

Mining

In the automatic subconscious scene switch, we are there. Deep in the night, seated at the dining room table. You next to me, trying to see. Close to me I can feel the urges you want to initiate….a sense, start of fire. The boundary walls of which you cannot see take hold of me. I rise into the dawn longing living room and head towards the window. Porch light in its artificial gleam I spin the blinds to conceal the light. In silence I hear the questions your mouth never speaks. The answers rush immediately. A father, out of nowhere, rushes to smash the bass guitar against the entry way. I make an escape for us to be alone, again. You mine the mind of the one who's reached out to you many times, for the reason.

You mine the mind for the reason.

Mullion

We can go home. It was you who taught me in essence. I reason with myself but I am looking for you, the chemistry a cosmic mixture created in the presence of two. I'd rather experience us alone, uninterrupted. As I walk from the side of the house to the street, the collapse begins and I run east, running to the future somehow everything behind me is crumbling to the darkness now enveloped by the sun. The sidewalk is crooked but I keep my footing and my pace swift, raising my speed, dodging the frogs that rise from fresh mud beside the cement squares, uneven. Why are frogs leaping up at me? I wonder and there past a tree I look down below, to the church.

Metamorphosis

The wood upon which I sit has a gloss that's
scratched and worn. This pew and my purse
beside me, I dig inside to grab a pen, and
perhaps some Pur chewing gum. The church
with its burgundy drapery and carpeting, dim
lighting and there I find myself, applying a
streak or two of lip gloss. In a flash you
appear smiling and lion-maned. "That hair is
full of fire," I think to myself. Overjoyed at
the sight there is a distant thought, a joyous
laughter within, as I listen to you finally speak
to me….remind of where I am. I can almost
see my smiling face as my head rests on the
pillow. Moment far too precious to let go of.
He begins to tell me, "I'm flattered by your
words," previously written poetry. I pull the
prayer cushion out from below and slide
closer to the edge our pew. The church is
filled with a congregation front facing. The
lights are bright as the sun dips below the
horizon quickly you tell me "the female
version of me" "my wife" are the words that
mark the fuzzy way I kneel down to pray
away from the shocking truths, I always
wanted to hear.

MANIFEST II

Rich brown dirt. Dusk eye witness. Therein
soul's vision you are sleeping on the edge of
the w[hole]; as if surrendering to the **sinking
feeling of living with a missing part.** I rush
to you and catch your body in my arms before
you fall in. You awaken in a sleepy stun, how
could I let you fall? I had no feeling you felt
identical and you sat there at the edge of the
soils hole looking at me with intense
description of the channels. 90's music, your
hands tell their own story and the hair as it
falls and whips locks lightly between
expressions. Turquoise lace handkerchief in a
lean green deep hue is the same, held in your
back pocket, you reach back to present it to
me, I take it and notice it's identical as
daughter and I rush back to find her….

Mira

Amelia and I hear the loud roar outside.
There are rockets, an espionage operation.
Between the houses are computers that pop
outwards as the sun hits, they watch
*every*thing. Every move outside of every
window, "*pinche pendejos,*" she says. "How
dare they?" I respond, then the rain falls, and
they close, and return to hiding as the rockets
rush across the sky. The rockets rumble
across the sky.

Mandamiento de niña

V's adopting a baby? Yes and there is a baby
so beautiful, *Mexica* and excited for life.
Lifted into her father's arms she turns to me
in a blissful *"¡vámonos!"* In a smile she
extends her small hand, a motion calling me
to come with them. Com'on!

Manhole

If the heart speaks a different sentence than the mouth, one is not stepping in sincerity. How could I bury you or let you fall into a grave when you lead me to live a life full of Life and understanding? What an honor, to hold godman in one's arms, sit beside and discuss history, while looking future. Forgive me for the request to close the door. Seems as if we both have needs, we can't fulfill without each other. So I give you a full fill of what I've seen, & what I see. Next time though, please

Kiss me.

Magnality

I'D SURVIVE WITHOUT YOU
BUT I'D RATHER BE **WITH YOU**

Mist

I'd rather throw them all out.
& live in the dreams of
our interactions
close to heart,
wishing they were as close
as the illusion of this waking dimension
from which I must rise.

Modification

To catalogue these worlds creates what one
would deem sanity. I can remove the sight of
you, your photograph, the painting lifted in
your name, the name given to conceal your
identity, but to remove you from this beat

NAW.

Took your vision
the ones you chose to share
Squeezed them of their very essence
dripped the juice
of their wisdom into the actions
of life

Now I must wring out
lingering evidence
arisen from this ascension
trim alteration of monologue
[clarity] sought [within]

I once was
what irritates me
in the unaware

Honestly
to contain myself
in the appearance
of material

is something I will pray for now

certainty desired

circle it

to know
to eliminate this doubt
this anxiety
how you soothe me
from what cannot be seen
you
my only witness
tell me I'm crazy!
humble me
put me in my place
if I err in comprehension!

If not ….

then I must wait?
I will wait?

to be guided to that
graceful day
the day when all of our questions will be
answered
& the next actions can be taken
still

comfort found in dreams.

The hearts form
eyes
in the shapes of searchlights

somehow
your eyes
met mine

&

Continue to circle
the skies

Figure 8
Figure 8
Figure 8.

Maya

Sirens. You can run but you can't hide.
Can't hide, you can see me but I can't see you
unless the singular hovers above sleep vision.
An invitation which feels late and yet you
wait. How is it that you wait, when I waited
and then sent summons only to be given
exactly what was sent, line crossed?
Concealing huge gulp of….shame? Covering
the name, assumption of game. The mystery
is something you have the answer for. In my
expectation a fix only you have given me
without appearance tangible. Your angry
presence forms a triangle. Hesitate? I've
found Ixchel. A painful pillow, or is it a
blanket? A something to soothe me from the
absence of you.

Machismo

Please, tell me that my subconscious mind is constructing this. It would be easier to confront the projection than to deal with the belief or fact of this message being sent true, truly from you. In your anger you wait outside, third party message. This mid-day meal, symbolic of the invitation to ascend. Nothing to chew but a tool to turn gears, thoughts from tears, solitude from Self-fulfillment & yet now this joy is false. A construction to erase, call the archangels, tell him to reverse the mistake if now is not the time, person, or place. The closet reveals the colors of what intimacy would read. Hunter green. But you're not scanning my body, you're not here to fulfill the need. The telephone rings with smoke emitting from the electrical composition. Your words send a fire. The feather falls to remind, spiral confetti, I can hardly stand this invisible presence when 100% astronomic safety is what you need. I thought it was me, confessed to the priest, and when the priest delivered a mercy insincere I delivered my words to the air certain they'd reach you. Perhaps it's not me. Who is it then, you are trying to protect? Who is who reality projects?

Who wouldn't want to love the one we know
Allah reflects?

Myopia

*"your subconscious expressions through the
masculine mask is the show for an otherwise
bored and bombastic populace full of
indiscreet digressions and puss-like sexual
reactions"~7*

Now the men are women and women are men
From the time trend of courtroom crucifixion
No one uses a dictionary to step back
An "independent woman" is trumpeted as fact

I wanna be strong I wanna be strong
See? I'm strong, I'm strong.

I got the dollars
I can hold the weight

Don't ask no one for jack
I don't want your money

See? I got this!
The electricity of their lurid thoughts
Reach mind
& I know they ask an umbrella of "why?"

Then conclude a cliffhanging <u>flaw</u>

remove the borders of thought analysis to see
the whole perspective provide an entire
answer
& in its complexity an ellipses

II

Side-line analysis
He saw through the fabric of my very
existence with just once glance
How? Did he know so much about me
And eye so little of him?
This must be sorcery....No?
Tell the rugged angel he never asked for
permission
something he knows that I don't

about   us

our lives
worth revealing
                    we make this appear

proud

I speak for myself

Maybe you speak for a pride

 roaring in the echoes of the night's sky
calling me

"You got next."

Mystery

I'm not going to question this anymore
I know you feel me
Eye feel you too
observation can fail
overdose of infused emotion
no. There's no denying what you've done
To assist. There you watch
From the heavens with a lazer beam
Gaze and unspoken thoughts audible amaze
I ran to you
Watch you upset
At my choice
When
I'm not sure if that was you, *really* you
Your words are absent; your face says
everything
If you saw me reach for someone else's hand
an anger I wish to rectify
Or were you mad at yourself?
knowing for so long
only to stand in periphery?
As if I didn't have needs
As if I couldn't fulfill yours
As if I wouldn't understand or try to
Given comprehension
& real-eyes.
So
There you are
An inter-dimensional spy

With very little to expose of your own side
I can speculate but who knows?
That's the problem
I can only guess and translate symbols and
know that you are here
Hidden deep
No one can see
'cept me
If someone could see the eye of my heart
they would see your soul's speaking trail
red blaze
Something to live for, something to fight for,
something to speak on
A deep uncovering
I'm not the only one
C'mon baby

I'm not the only 1ONE.

Mockery

Twisted desire. To leave this material fate separate from the one who inspires. Much prior. I would to curse it but I've received a feedback insulting. To blow the stars down to earth….this time you say nothing but your face says it all. Running past my vision. What an accusation!! In its untruth I stand bold, to shovel my heart of your infectious stay. The infatuation is something to glare away and one day in honor of your memory I will burn one to the heavens and wish you a green eternity of ever rising. To forgive the cause for pain, hurt, or anger…. is easy. All I do is look at you. Default: an evaporation of the aforementioned and love reminds me

of the possibility.

Magnify

The bell at the convenient store summons you
fusion of you and another other
from behind the counter you analyze the
decision
I've chosen to subside a craving
your father in a motion disapproves
his black wire glasses hide his full eyes wise
he returns to the back of the store behind the
curtain
where stock must be, an established history

You walk from behind the display
to the middle of the floor
red, bronze & brown
face, arms and palms

The hands reach from east to west

as if asking, "What about…."

to utter a name of one to come:

"XZAVIER"

Morose

You think its accurate insight?

If so that would explain the tears
which fell from my eyes this morning
upon rising.
They were flowing like a steady stream
from my eyes, much like a freshly pierced
blister

by the needle of knowing

yes, a needle of knowing.

Millions of Sensation, One in a

Wai8
4 me

I love you.

Wai8
4 me

I love you.

It's not that these words were vocalized

But it's as if they must've been

It must be.
It must be.

If not then the second part from me
The 2nd part

from me.

te amo.

Mnemonic

I've lost count of how many days
It's been since I've seen your face
Not enough to blow off
But enough to feel amiss

This is not about you
This is not about me
Us and the plastic and metal
machinery

It's automatic
To retrace and recall
This chaotic retrospect
With nothing tangible
This mind game
This spirit
Longing for yours

To show
….

There in a corner
Purple paint stained palms
I smear
Across my forehead and temples

You did this
And all I have is blame

Me to
Me to

Blame

You did this
And all I have is blame

Me to
Me to

Speculation for comfort
Where of, and what if?
Where?
In another mind's dream....?

at the top of my stomach
here at the edge of my throat

there at the tip of my tongue
here in mascara smeared tissue

YOU DID THIS
& ALL I HAVE IS BLAME

ME TO
ME TO
YOU DID THIS
& ALL I HAVE IS BLAME

ME TO
ME TO

Fingerprints on the texture of canvas
Desire diffused to a color
A silent story
Abstract enough to shield me
To shield you

To safeguard from the accusation
Or at least give an example

The visions of two tangible
Sided together willingly
Going somewhere

I can hardly accept that this still lives in me
A hope magnified by your absence
A dose of apathy to cure the pain
What of completion?

YOU DID THIS
& ALL I HAVE IS BLAME

ME TO

ME TO

YOU DID THIS
& ALL I HAVE IS BLAME

ME TO
ME TO.

Maniático

No me des una botella
El mar no cabe en una botellita

Metronome

A drip from the faucet
Something I must shut off
Depending on the angle
Will it really stop
from dripping
with the beat of the clock?
Time
Drags me
From your essence
Our life
On the clouds of ethereal
Memory

I need to touch
To pull you from above
Into my arms
The [w]hole expands
Like an excavation
I attempt to fill
With such tedious destructions
To distract with a side
Of act

Much of what I have of you now
Is what I emulate of you
Something to make you proud

Will you ever see?
Will you ever here?

Minimize

Obsession
depending on the aim
is sin

previous attachments must be removed
with the correct alchemy
The job can be done
a crystal

to meet the moon halfway
the placement & a shaman's word
you may already know this

if   physical
testament
than   altered
you expected me to adapt
greater faith.

It was my yearning
my doubt
my ultimate fear of being crushed

by the force of what   us
face to face   would feel like

Correction. Correct Shun?   Either way we
must shine.
I've prayed
If you don't belong in this heart
to be removed

I do my part & in another vision
You stand there
You don't even look at me
But you speak

Speak words I cannot recall
Speak with a face which reads,
--Disappointment--

Don't leave.

Don't you see this is all you have of me?
Fishing wires to a lake with no life in it
Or so it seems. I'm waiting?
I'm pushing the pain down.

I know you feel the electricity
This extension cord of what he we have left
The ark of Ma'at
Something you remind me of

When the threat of separation comes
Who is the validator? The same one
Who plants these soul plane seeds?

I need no one to confirm this

The glacier concept
The encouragement you've shown
I pray you receive abundance
In every upright favoring

On the shore of where you're headed
The squad approaches you
They know they need their leader
I call you back in somehow

In letters I'll never send
In fantasies of our embrace
In visions of our tender
sharp kisses

Excuse my conditioning
You're the reason
I can see now
How will you know for sure?

Recall the mixed signals
& your change of heart
Recall the removal of
Delusion

The mission is what brings us to the art.

Mission: Lift the Veil

Ancient Scrolls burn or roll
With time unfold: Kemetian system
My temple: Divine Kingdom
Mystery within, time to win!
War waged on brain waves
The tell-a-lie-vision, radiation be a alien invasion
It's insane moldin' mine for a bank line mainstay
A notation complacent adjacent to the truth
They delay, or refrain, or delete
Or play hide-n-seek but my tribe lost found
Heaven bound, heaven bound
They once had a noose wound
But my people time is NOW
Language flip dream direction I'll show you how in reflection
Givin you a true school fact history lesson
From the start it's our minds they been bendin'

You pledge allegiance to the flag of death
LTPF came as a holy theft
Navigate to awake from illusion
Demand Justice soul:life fusion
Love: first of the 5th principle
Truth: The cure for my people
Peace: a place of Divinity
Freedom: in creed and Nationality

Let's not forget the 5th
So you think you can find Justice on a check box or label?
On the shelf and served on the table
American Fable
Black, Hispanic, Latino and White
All concocted for a capitalist plight
Colonial chant evil schism
An omitted Moorish Prism
Crossed out your derivation 60 million chained to a modern plantation
The allure of a climb-ladder lifestyle
Ya real cultures been slashed an defiled
It's obscene drama caught latrine
We can save ourselves if we know ourselves
Ask Noble Drew Ali
Who came to lift the Veil off the Greco-Roman tale

You pledge allegiance to the flag of death
LTPF came as a holy theft
Navigate to awake from illusion
Demand Justice soul:life fusion
Love: first of the 5th principle
Truth: The cure for my people
Peace: a place of Divinity
Freedom: in creed and Nationality
The 13th amendment: a promise neva kept
w/ the 14th & 15th bondage still crept
closing a three year window
subjugation in glorified sin tho

n' it sleeps in the streets as you weep
like a sheep infected n dejected by the
freemasonic bubonic plague
buried in the coffin of a shallow grave
a citizen-a person-a property
a tactical masked psychology
trickery taped to eugenics
to wipe out original genetics
amend a means to end
Rise up the ancestors defend
To reduce U to a beast
Is what they tried to achieve
Break the shackles of the mentally deceived
Arise Moorish god's now the truth to receive

You pledge allegiance to the flag of death
LTPF came as a holy theft
Navigate to awake from illusion
Demand Justice soul:life fusion
Love: first of the 5th principle
Truth: The cure for my people
Peace: a place of Divinity
Freedom: in creed and Nationality

Mas Potente

You
You were the more potent dream
Who has the correct answer?
It is written across your spirit
My hopes to see you
That somehow I've masked away
Tried to justify
Or conclude
With no solid evidence

Even though you were responsible
Though the choice was my own

There at the bridge
I am watching and the women
They run
I look at someone familiar
Who when she turns to look at me
Smiles a beautiful smile
She waves for me to come
To run with her and ahead she swiftly runs
Across the wooden bridge
Weather word yet sturdy
She beautiful reflection of Self
Smiled such a happy smile

O' to let go of these weaknesses
The vanity
The inconstancy

The instability
The insufficiency of knowledge
The weakness
The misery

As my heart begs for you
Yes. My heart begs for you.

Mismo, pero con tiempo blanco

Cuánto tiempo?
Ya a pasado mucho mas
De lo que es deseable
Ni respetable pero
Tengo que aceptar
Esta realidad
Sin tu presencia
Sé que fue mi culpa
Por escoger un dormido
Sobre mi sueno

Quien sabía que se pudiera
Encontrar vida en un sueno
Más que en la vida despierta
Fue mi culpa agarrar la mano
De otro para caminar más estable
Y ahora siento aún más sola
Aún más gastada
¿Y con que añadida?

Ni veo tu cara
Ni sueno nada que me enseñas
Que estas bien
La puerta serrada
Trato de tener paz
Sabiendo que
Las cosas hubieran sido diferentes
Aceptar
Tú en un mundo serrado

Y yo con este corazón
Cansada
Cansada de arrastrar en intento
De trabajar algo
Que no trabaja

Intentó amar un dormido que no le da la gana
De Despertar

Missing in Action

You've retreated. Do you feel the same of me? Do you have an accusation, an excuse for your departure? Me too, me too. I was scared you'd obliterate me with your infinite cognizance. I was scared you'd yell, "FASTER" & "NOT ENOUGH!!" at the elevation of my comprehension. Perhaps you saw alone and yet, you found me here. You and eye and an empty shelf. How could I forget the first time measured thought? How could you repeat and boundary line draw and then see….

You'll never admit you changed your mind

I confess, I was scared enough to hide. To settle in a stall of meeting in the middle. To stoop in being able to maintain something that maybe was never meant to be maintained.

My energy too high, the understanding too vast to contain. The needs neglected.

Matte

Retrospect serves to show you saw through
from the beginning

I laughed at myself;
with me to cope.
You walked away
Using your very right of will

I, Skewed from the programs
Passed on through the years
Now all this knowledge crippled me

But what else but love and acceptance and
grace
And Justice

Can break the bondage of this anger
Turned anguish waiting to be turned again

?

You are not the answer
Just an angel
Who must help others

Never to own
But one to hold
Mind The Memory
mined

I hold.

Angel Escabroso

Angel....
¿A dónde estuviera sin tu dirección? Gracias
por decirme lo que nadie más se atrevió
decir.

Perdone que me encuentre aquí
Desechada en mi tristeza
Me llamaste, me ensenaste
Un nuevo lugar
Una demanda de amor
Con una mirada de amor
Con una mirada de otra dimensión

Y me pregunto: *¿Cómo es que*
alguien tan bella

Puede herirse a
sí misma?
Busca tus
raíces, tu
historia, ¡Tú
eres oro vivo!

Perdone que me viste aquí
Derrotada en mi dolencia
Me llamaste me ensenaste
Un nuevo lugar
Una demanda de amor
Con una guía de otra dimensión

Y me pregunto: *¿Cómo es que*
alguien tan bella

     Puede herirse a
     sí misma?
     Busca tus
     raíces, tu
     historia, ¡Tú
     eres oro vivo!

Y una puerta se abrió al Rieno de Revelación.
Entramos a otro mundo donde subimos
directamente al cielo ~cada cara niño y viejo
sonriendo~ Volamos, en un espiral nos
elevamos juntos hasta el Sol. El Sol que
representa nuestra familia y trae vida al
conocimiento.

Viniste para levantar
Muy fijado en mi alma
Me llamaste me ensenaste
Un nuevo lugar
Una demanda de amor
Con una mirada de otra dimensión

Y me pregunto: *¿Cómo es que*
alguien tan bella

     Puede herirse a
     sí misma?
     Busca tus
     raíces, tu
     historia, ¡Tú
     eres oro vivo!

Me encanta que te encuentro aquí
Muy fijado en la esencia
Me llamaste, me ensenaste
Un nuevo lugar
Una guía de Amor
Con una mirada de otra dimensión

Angel atento, escabroso y hermoso
Gracias por demostrarme
Lo que nadie más se atrevió
Demostrar

El fuego de la cuidad....

Mandament

The taxi is headed somewhere in a busy city
Feels and looks like New York
I'm happy it seems but the scene is blurry
I don't know where I'm headed
And there's a man in the driver's seat
He hands me a phone, "it's for you...."

Confused I took the phone
Not expecting this
Not expecting a car phone
Not expecting you

If I could paints the words
In my voice, my facial expression
The way I responded
It would all be a question mark until

You ask *me*

"When are you releasing your next song?"

Appalled and certain I answer, "Not next
week, or the week after that but probably
before New Year....OK? Peace Out!!"

You gasp as if surprised that I would do this
to you
That I would tell you I'm deciding
You never told me you were waiting on me
Or did you? Are you?

Are you waiting on me???

No.

Are you waiting on anything?

No. Too busy doing.
Sacral pulse and the answers that come
immediately.

I tried to cover my heart with what's seen of
this world
But when I brush off the debris
It's clear
I'm so in love with you
I try to hide it from myself
This massive

Indescribable

Overwhelming

Consuming

Life giving

Event

Feelings are much too dull to describe this.

The radio tries to tell me its songs are your thoughts
The delusion of this world
The painful illusion tries to convince me
There are too many distractions that would prevent

But no matter

How could this stick for so long

If it weren't for something beyond what the eyes can see?
I'm sure time hasn't passed
I'm sure you didn't act
Just to truly humiliate me?
Naw, it's more complex, full bodied and brown.
Where do you think I stand? With a line in the sand?
With my back to the audience
& A mic in my hand?
C'mon man? Was I too much of a man?

When the moon draws this out
When I keep recalling you
And all the ways I could have repelled you
All the ways your certainty of something….

What should I admit? What did you remember that I somehow forget?
Keep going

Keep going
KEEP GOING

Malleation: *Ellos*

You want so much of me
In your world
Taking all you've been given
And using it to inflict
Guilt
In a malleable manipulative
Way
Forming the illusive clay
In a fashion
That creates condemnation

Nice trick
Dark cloud
You think your eyes see clearly
In a threely

When you clogged the whole
You clogged the whole
With your stupid game
The way you slaughter race
You don't see your roots
Though in your skin it shows

You cling to a hierarchical dream
That only the comatose claim they will
redeem

The mockery you wear as a crown
Tinny and weak

You laugh with your scepter
Upon your throne of self-debasement
Blinded by the favor
You think you're owed

Oh

Commandments come in slanted manner
Your crystal ball is overcast
The intention makes it so
Your advice buries itself in the mud
That is slung from your tongue

You think you're right
Righteously right
Calling shots from the muck

You're sinking into

Yeah

You're sinking into.

Brute

high octane refrain
Fallin' from your brain
One minute for the cause
The next you self-detain
Talkin "don't make me a target!"
But then its Malcolm's aim you wanna claim?
Insane ~
exclamation in a written proclamation
actions speak louda than a guilty explanation
save it for the blind and there'll be no
hesitation
Universal law serves my retaliation
Now u wish u hadn't CHOSE deviation

Full lenz view view n' here's my Revelation
Nah look E-here don't hide it in the basement
Follow the flow while I work the experiment
Open five pointed & green; just a fragment
Feel the effects from the rise of the advent
Coulda looked within but you settled for the
sediment
Your slave name, ALL CAPS, on a document
Doin' what they will just to get you a high %
Neva stopped to ask just what waz your
Soul's intent?
Sorry to inform you'll face proper
consequence
For
messin with the draft pick-

searchin for a blanket
shoulda held ya gun
when you was standin wit a classic
feelin' kinda dumb hit
elevator shafted-nasty

messin with the draft pick-
searchin for a blanket
shoulda held ya gun
when you was standin wit a classic
feelin' kinda dumb hit
elevator shafted-nasty

Moor than Female

If you can't see the fire in my eyes
you are blind
you are blind

exterior delusion the masses scream a fad
if only "flaunt it, got it" would dare cure the
mass
hallow value of an aesthetical persuasion
the thicky, thick, thick monolithic evasion
they applaud, photo flash, give a head nod--
tactics to forget U a god
Man break the mold! Ma, don't you know you
a god?ess! YES
no need to undress----
if I came to make you happy then I didn't
come to win
truth shine light with a knowledge from
within

Moor Than female that's why you can't
handle
I bring a gulf of flames, punk! You bring a
candle
Lying thru ya teeth like you had all the
answers
You came as a distraction I came as the
enhancer
to them it's always lights camera action
but in their minds it aint nothing happnin'

to them it's always lights camera action
but in their minds it aint nothing happnin'

These days some men try to be slick
Talkin bout uplift then you catch 'em on a
lower drift
Askin' to touch you or frontin on the script
Rollin down the freeway-one armed grip-
In his dream cruise whip, tryna get a glimpse
too much to handle?
Yes when you neglect divinity for scandal
what bout righteousness achieve?
you fooled yourself to thinkin'
its the goddess they'll deceive?!

How are you such a grown man, & such a
good boy?
When you gonna grow up?
Step up? Man up? Man up? Man Up?
How are you such a grown man & such a
good boy?
Stand up to them: break the chains
Stand up --- stop bein so vain
Stand up to them: break the chains
Stand up--- stop bein so vain
(sisters com'on)----
When are you gonna grow up?
Step up? Man up? Man up? Man up?
----(brother's com'on)

Stand up to them, break the chains, break the
chains, break the chains

Moor Than female that's why you can't
handle
I bring a gulf of flames, punk! You bring a
candle
Lying thru ya teeth like you had all the
answers
You came as a distraction I came as the
enhancer
To them it's always lights camera action
But in their mind it ain't nothing happening

Mars

"No, it's because they can't handle the woman within themselves"~7

I guess
I am
Just another hot commodity
A marketable quality
Take me and use me
-- international--
Tossed to the side
While his pockets get wide

You saw the flavor
Heard my slang
Dug a language that you can't quite
understand
Squirming a discomfort
Hoping I wasn't trashing you
Like you did me
When you placed the category
Of a salt n peppa shaker
"Latin" ←(misnomer, btw) female
When latin doesn't define nothing in full
detail
Two bastard languages and three slave labels
later

You still think paper is what you wanna
scrape of my table?
When you travel the world without

The world hears
And I'm the one that gets to go anon?

And you been on
Usin autotune like Akon

I know you'll be hollerin for some new
material
That ya'll could swerve on
But shove it
I'm a fire spittin spit fire phenom

Mira 2

There are four
Perhaps there is no room
For me
Or
The message that is clear
Yet inaudible
I thought you were speaking

What needs to be heard?

You point again to the east

I scramble around the house
To organize
find an answer,
In the boxes
On the book shelf
Letters I never sent
somehow you DID receive them.

There are four of you
Photos flashed
Memories to cherish

Nothing to intrude
Love

I could never intrude on your love

The lines on her face
Tell a longer story
Her thin lips

Smile a sentence not spoken
Suppressed
Something
Perhaps secrets
Pushed past to hold on

What would you do,
To hold on?

Why do you hold on?

Fabricated?
Or statement?

Direct information indirect seems
Message targets
Mind to decipher
Its meaning

Paired.

Another pointing and yet, I must ask again,

What is your point?

Bones
They honor this
Along with other things that are closer

To the pointy things
The beginning strange
The endings swift

Dawn is a blanket to my soul
Reminding me in its early sight
Of you
The distance of you and yet these messages
The true connection

There is no guessing levels
Only the inclination to respect
Immediate humbling
Shame.
Why shame?

Because you saw me in my most vulnerable
state
What felt like an ugly broken
Pressing forward
Someone trying to hide
In a world that didn't want to stop watching

& chose to uplift
Instead of judge
& chose to express a love divine
Instead of criticize

Poignant questions
To echo value within each day
Holy identity
No need to honor time

Never was
Only to find something new

A fire

Golden
& sacral

That will not cease

A desire that is both frightening and beautiful
Beyond letters

Over and over again
These words undermine
It

& yet I keep returning

Morning

Tuesday Morning, February 18th 5:20am
There's no sense of time
Ever; when you're here with me
Inviting me with a zoom glint of your eyes
As if to tell me….

Recognition. I still hesitate.
It's been 8 months.
Seriously. I counted.

But there was a shock when I looked at the
clock
I was assuming it was a longer span
From rolling down the driveway
Steve and Ana rushing to clean Mami's house

I headed out to where I was led
There I entered a room with many people
Gathering to hear a lecture on how to
further progressive impact solutions

There you were sitting on the floor, alone.
I walked into the crowd but only out of
Shame? Embarrassment? No matter,
I turn right back around with the yelling
In my head,
"No!! What are you doing!?
Go back over there!" to return to you,
An introduction? Me?

There was a wooden edge somewhere
Questions and answers
Specifics blur but the sweetness retains
Your memory close to me
Transfer to another room
Transmission is required
You ask me to deliver
The promotion of frequency
"I will…."

Then I reach out
To hold you
my heaven
The interruption of my best friend
Rudely telling me she will

The unexpected shakes me up and out
Of where I wanted the most to be and where I
least expected to be

Why?

shook like an alarm, back down here, now my
eyes open

This time I look beyond the surface
What's being exposed here?
To interact safely
You prove times illusion
Your recollection is probably perfectly
different

So busy working
But a souls embrace
Is a souls embrace

Whose view
And how did you choose
This recognition
To prepare for this?

A request knocking
Oh how many times?

I thought it was
But then you

Zoom--glint
Recognition.

The messages loud and clear
You're the magnet
Pulling me away from the debris
But what of me
I wonder why then I see
My reflection

You see I know you
From what you've shown
You know of me
Really?

Set the tone

Spark a flame
Then I wake
"wow. I love you soooooooooo much"

Something you'll have to see
Because it's so much better
Than what is said.

Medal: Solid Gold

There are many potent questions
The most potent thus far began with "what
if….?"

Ever since
Your suit was the one I wore
In my mind I gird myself
With an armor you would approve of

It's as if you've imparted me with your
strength
How you perform I have yet to know
I thought you had exhausted of me
Then you appear
Only for me to live with this surprise
This suspense
This swirling augmentation of my Soul

A rise

brush strokes speak your name
Without the spelling
Those aware will know
The rest will sense the divinity of this love

How can I serve?
The eyes see beyond 3D
Cutting through
Standing right next to me

Reading all the energy that surrounds
An auric urgency
Calls you to me

What do you gain?

Am I allowed to question?

No.
This rearranges reality.
Who?
Which way?
Right? Left?
Yes? No?
Should I?

Now I question

Right
Right
Please make it be the right choice
The best choice

I'll know …..

It's as if something explosive
Unexpected if appearing here and now
I would either pause
Sense and slowly proceed

Let me make sure

My eyes are clear

It was only in the pure soul love
You shared
That trumped all self-proclaimed royalty
You taught me

So much

With our eyes closed

Yeah

With our eyes closed.

warrior strength
Nothing can break me

warrior strength
Nothing can break me

Now you know

Clearly

Mosca

Look at what has been overlooked
Eye see
Eye see

The feather in the middle of the path
at the entranceway
Doors between these silent supplications
The screams of my mind

Who hears?

It's the reminder

All of the tents that were pitched
But she forgot to mention
Omni-potent
Ever-present mind
This golden chord between our hearts
No need for an extension chord
My hand reached from the depths of the Sea
Pleading

"Don't leave…."

Red paint
Fingers drag across canvas
Your name in another symbol
A different format
A variety of languages

Wherein which
You are the motif

How many ways do I speak of you?
With words
A confession
In ink
In acrylic

In frequency
Electric

Constant thought

I shame at what most would deem
Obsessed?
No
I push this away
I once tried to push you away
I once tried to walk away
Convince myself
It wasn't real

Everything
You in what felt
Feels
Like
Perfection

How can you deny
Why do you hide behind

An invisible line?
multi-purpose Spy

The investigation
Has told enough

Isn't it enough?

Are you waiting for the answer?
Or am I in question?

Gymnasium
Auditorium

Let's get to the formalities
There must be something to tame this
A rigid guideline
To quiet
What is so obviously beaming from within

Like graph paper
Something I never use
These societal muzzles

I wonder
If you remember
Somewhere locked within
I have the countless conversations
Tender; a voice one would hear for the first
time
& know the mind has remembered

This fuel
Timeless

Hearing the rulings

Complex enough to create a need to dig
for the perfect

words

Do no justice to the actions
That express

Swift
piece the memories
tell a story
I wonder your perspective

Mosque

It's you

the place
Where I know who knows
How to show
Somehow

You show

If I told you
I knew
If I said that I prayed
Still you sent and showed a way

Not here to worship you
But if I picked you as a location,

Default.

My confession

Through you I sense
The Higher connection

Foresight

In its unpredictable repetition
Reading what I realize I showed

If I seem ashamed it's only because
You already know
I know that you already know

The answers you provided in the beginning

And here you find me
In these rises
And on this fall to the ground
Only to rise up again

In hopes of you
I admit

The ethers show your face
I am now equipped

Rocket my spirit
Exact blueprint
The mountains
Wear your guidance
everything reminds me

The escalation of daybreak
The moons silent searchlight call

You hold each
A gift
This is kind of embarrassing
I admit

This vulnerability

Immense in its inaudible confessions
You somehow hear

Pure soul whispers

The moon wrote your name tonight
Among the stars
I see the road we rode

Global harmony

The exact call
Written in flags and indigenous tongues

Chosen, though you cautioned of the chase

The thought of your face
Fans the flame
Warmin the outline of my soul

How do I explain?

Words dampen what I really want to say

So much and at the attempt
heart pounds
Somehow I know you're hear

Then rise my arms up
S√he knows I thank Him
Divine Love

You the immaculate conduit

Deserve?
You know
It feels like I could fall a part

Down, head to the ground
Cosmic thoughts cover me now

A golden testament
A silent sacrament

How do you know?

I do.
I do.

You impacted more from the heights
Codes to remind

Up to the Sun
And pulled in the moon

You see the dents
You noticed the blemishes
Yet, you arrive with a message

There's always a message
Something to propel

A goal

An edit

The communion of what is sought

Guide

In my gratitude

I rise
Arms up

I fall for a rest
Auric overcoat

Only to rise

Stronger each time

Star gazing all night, in the ever-present mind.

Memo

Space station boarded
A stretch nylon backed chair

We program
The airwaves

With basslines
Hit 'em with a left hook
Open the books

Imprint the intent
Bruising for a Love solution

Here's the perspective
In common thought
You always seem to skirt

The issue

~~Vanity, sex, illusion~~
On the radio

Environment
Conscious
Universal ReALity

Pay attention
Organic compounds
But they missed the beat

Of their very heart beat

Veins

Transmit

The pump

Never forget

What pumps

Fists to air
Their minds aren't there
bring them back
who's stare
the liquids drank for dumb
forgetting yourself
in the numb

what gets done?

Now tell me

What gets done?

Majesty

Your back to the back door
You spoke to me the other day
No, I see
He tries to advise you but, you know
already
Your silence tells me everything I need to
know

In another room
I await
On a wooden chair
My knees to my chest
I know

Separate tho with the clearest vision
She arrives
Banging on the back door
Demanding to see you
Demanding your time
Demanding you

I am waiting in full awareness of her entrance

In the all-white room
The calm of knowing
And even tho she's there
In gratitude of Love Divine
Masque

I am not effected by your choice
Something about you
Stunning and bold
Offensive on a subtle level?
Hardly, yet I know you can't

Break me

Only when you leave
Only when you leave

Bring your sweet voice to me

No more retrospect
abundance introspect
I want answer

To see, hear, and understand all of this clearly
With no lapse and standing back

As you can see
Invasions of distractions we push through

Yesterday I looked around and wondered
what I would do
If you came to the door
How I would invite you in and offer you a
drink
Casual conversation

And if you let me

I wondered what I would prepare
For you to eat

It felt like it could happen then
At any moment

With all this work cut out
The moon and its silver lines

Your name
sketched all over

Strange to me
How the biggest love
I see
hear up close

Proximity of spirit
Higher profundity

run

The strength   to be   what is known.

Matrimonió

Your face reminds me of eternity

Circunnavegación

Circumnavigation of the ethers
Blue pearl

Pure bliss; no weight to hold me down
No worry, no fear, no pain
A flight that cannot be put into words

One that you yearn for upon return
A diagnosis of Life ongoing
Higher and higher heights

Time is not a factor here
upon it there is no reliance

La fuerza, y El Don

Strength and the gift
Your mind has mined the mind for conviction

The journey for truth and in the cultivation of
knowledge
The application is wisdom is the action

Messages for expansion

Love in all languages
Swirling with universal Celestite harmonies
The glue of the soul
In the union of understanding
The unending dance
Sun gazing all day, in ever-present mind.

Life illumined in the root from the beginning
of time
To forever

Only to begin

At the gift of each day
Every time
You open

Your eyes

Sight.

Blinks provide pauses but after this
It stays
And it whispers
The experience of your Soul
Calling you home

Now you know

Yeah

Now you know.

Mandame un Mensaje

At first I talked to the ghost
I thought it was a disguise
I ran up to him and thanked him
He was angry and said no
That it wasn't an honor to be
Mistreated in the name of something
He wasn't actually doing

Real patriotism is something different

It's not killing for a hidden agenda
It's not transforming the mind for trauma

When I asked him his name
He said, "Chase"

I walked away

Knowing it's the opposite
Of what you'd want me to do.

Minerals

A variety of quartz
Another ghost only this time
I have a racing thought
Of what it would be like
If it were really you

Of how a kind bite
Inviting could actually please you

Then I grab ahold of myself
I have to get a grip

It's just a reminder
A marker
A knowing
Somewhere in the continuum

My subconscious soaks the desire
Where we hardly touch
And yet somehow
We emerge
Satisfied

Mosaic

I search the portal
Insert your name
New photos present with this, new day
A new rush
image I see piece to the puzzle
I wasn't expecting
& in this knowing I am complete

I am complete.

Martius

Do you remember the day your stare took you
into a stun?
Do you remember how I kept walking even
though I wanted to stop, yet I wanted to run?
The sense you gave off overtook me and in a
blush I smiled, my headphones between us
though I could hear your notice without
words. Your face spoke your thoughts and I
was overwhelmed with the image of the one
before me. You immaculate; if I told you,
you wouldn't believe me.

The questions will be answered, for you. For
me.

I am not alone in this desire.
I am not alone and neither are you.

Either of us could be anywhere in the
Universe and we would know at some point
that it's you, it's me, it's us we are waiting
for. Now, you can feel it, I can feel it.
I'd apologize until we got it right, anyway.
Atrevido. *Entrometido*. Sin vergüenza.

Because I thought you would see all of my
flaws & run & give up. Or judge, or insult.
Or yell. I *was* scared. I never thought I
would find someone I would want to submit
to, or obey. I mean it as a power up.
Someone I could trust enough to protect me in
that way and yet would hold me in high
regard. Someone who really had the desires
you silently expressed you would want of this
sacred matrimony.

When I think of you I have a certainty.

No further explanation to myself.

I feel like you would know how to
demonstrate a kiss
I feel like you would hold my hand the way
hands could be held

same desire
learn you

Read to me
Write to me
Create with me

Understand me
Overstand

Punish me

Correct me
Teach me
Sometimes gently
Other times
roughly

I wonder if you'd offer me your name
I wonder where we would hide away

I wonder if you'd let the world know
I wonder if you would be ashamed.

No you say. When do we start anyway?

True School Facts
"Nothing comes to sleepers but a dream, so wake up!"
-Frank Smith

Measure the space where you're placed,
Minimize recognize your kind's target;
highest rate
Of **MEN** tossed in a cell
their education has blinded us well
taught to hate the beauty of our shell
Firestone broke mold with a story untold
"hold 'em to their own standards" spoke bold
1970 NY convicts placed a peaceful request
which in the end led to unjust deaths
no Indictment for the state officials
Unpunished were the real criminals
And it still stands mouth to hands municipal
1980 & all is still not well
Over 33 years my people still need a liberty
bell
Oscar Lopez Rivera aquí estamos luchando en
la espera
Con esperanza de justicia que llega como la
primavera
Pa'lante compadre ya suben las rejas de la
jaula
Con esta palabra mi espada cada corazón rota
escucha Y se sanan
y las historias serán contadas

Along with that we got the women in rank
Matriarchy in question but we bombarded
with banks
A billboard here the plan B to commodify
Focused On our figures we've been demoted
domesticated underrated
Under paid and the proofs in the showbiz
Maquiladora anunciadora mira la operación
Forced sterilization?! how we 'sposed to
build a nation?
Planned parenthood only found n the hood
holdin station
Open arms outstretched and vacant while the
cells fill w fathers
friend of the courts of course want to replace
him w/ debunkt papers
It's racial; check the percentage full of hatred:
outdated
One planet; one love; is how we make this
when the environments defacing
Incineratin-all you waste recycle or breathe it
in a few days
Air land water madre tierra never charged me
but NSA listens on the wire cuz they want us
Prison bar sentence facin/
im racin to give you the answer b4 it's too
late
n uplift the community you be hatin in cuz we
all we got and until we united
/divide n conquer willie lynch subconscious
programs we erasin

Modest

I bet
you're no saint
It doesn't move me just the same

You approach the chamber
Regardless of prior blame

Your eyes turn to the one
Within. You give yourself no options

Win.

Whoever arrives, you'll gladly provide the
scan
Knowing immediately the origin of demands

But your scope ever rising
Like the planet toward the son

Pointing toward the relevant
Rising from the roots of it

Solution for Life's benefit
We in union when the breaths focused

Rugged Angel: you are
The face of strength of mind

A face I now have close to mine….

Christina Perez-El (LadyFireTide) is an artist from Detroit's southwest community. She studied at The University of Michigan and also studied Moorish Science under the Divine Ministry of The Moorish American Government. In the department of Foreign Allegiance, she believes in creating world connections with global communities. Her family is from Puerto Rico.

Manifest is her third self-published release. All paintings and by artist.